IMAGES
of England

AROUND
NORTH SHIELDS
THE SECOND SELECTION

Captain William Linskill, first Mayor of Tynemouth and developer of the north-east edge of North Shields.

IMAGES
of England

AROUND
NORTH SHIELDS
THE SECOND SELECTION

Compiled by
Eric Hollerton

TEMPUS

First published 2000
Copyright © North Tyneside Libraries, 2000

Tempus Publishing Limited
The Mill, Brimscombe Port,
Stroud, Gloucestershire, GL5 2QG

ISBN 0 7524 2157 3

Typesetting and origination by
Tempus Publishing Limited
Printed in Great Britain by
Midway Clark Printing, Wiltshire

The County Borough of Tynemouth Housing Committee inspecting the new housing estate to the west of North Shields.

Contents

Acknowledgements

Thanks are due to all those members of the public who have provided pictures or information to the Local Studies Centre of North Tyneside Libraries. Among those who helped are Mr C. Allan, Mr Brown, Mr Cessford, Mr Clay, Miss Conaty, Mr Dawson, Mr R.T. Dix, Mr Dowse, Mr Elliott, Mrs S. Ellis, Mr Elsdon, Mr Furness, Mr Gray, Mr Hogan, Mr Jones, Mr J.C. Lane, Prof. N. McCord, Robert McVay, Miss L. Miller, Mr Milne, Mrs Mitchell, Mrs Patterson, Mr V. Percy, Mr S. Rickard, Mr Robson, Mrs S. Ross, Mrs Nancy Sadler, Mr Scorer, Mr Scott (North Shields), Mr Scott (Whitley Bay), Mr J. Scott, Miss Sewell, Mr I.J. Smith, Mr Jack Smurthwaite, Mr Stephenson, Mr Stockdale, Miss D. Thompson, Mrs Walter, Mrs Walton, Mrs E. Watson, Mr H. Weir, Mr Wilkinson, Mr Woodhouse. Many of the photographs were taken by Roland Park, for various aspects of the work of the Tynemouth Borough Surveyor.

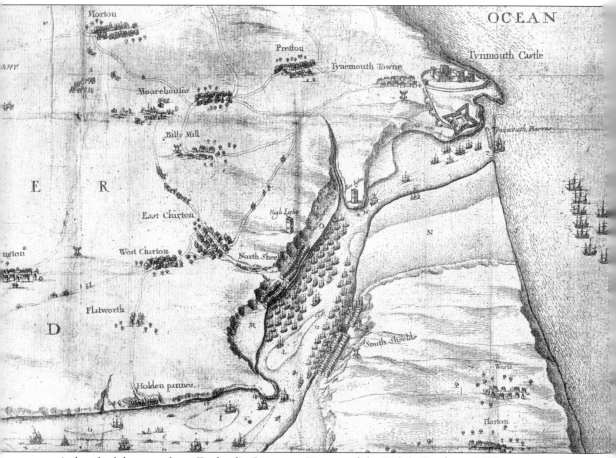

A detail of the map from *England's Grievance Discovered*, by Ralph Gardner, 1655.

Introduction

Even before the Norman Conquest the monastery at Tynemouth was supported by grants of land in the surrounding area. The house had been all but abandoned in the eleventh century, but ecclesiastical control of the area would have been considerable, particularly between 1075 and 1080, when Bishop Walcher of Durham was also Earl of Northumberland. Following a dispute with a later bishop, Robert de Mowbray, Earl of Northumberland, invited the Benedictine monastery at St Albans to take control at Tynemouth. Monks began to arrive on 26 October 1083. The Earl made an extensive grant of land, and the priors acquired more in later centuries.

From the twelfth century most of Tynemouthshire was held as a liberty of the Priory at Tynemouth. It was divided into the inshire and outshire. The former included the townships of Tynemouth, Milnetown with Shields, East, Middle and West Chirton, Flatworth, Murton and Preston. Around 1225 Prior Germanus began to develop the industrial town of North Shields, which led to centuries of struggle with the city of Newcastle. The rest of the inshire, however, seems not to have roused such animosity, despite the fact that there was considerable economic activity in the area. On the other hand, it did not always remain unscathed: a Scottish army is alleged to have burnt the whole of the shire in 1342. In the thirteenth century coal seams near the surface were widely worked, either by the monks themselves or by licensees. The locations of most of the pits are lost. Coal supported salt manufacture, which was got by boiling water from the River Tyne. The collieries of the Chirtons and Preston were surrounded by farms raising cereals and livestock. The latter also supported the tan-yards at Preston. The Murton area seems to have been less fortunate, being described at one time as a bleak moor. On the edge of the moor was one of a number of windmills under the control of the Priory. In a grant of 1320 it was referred to as Billing's Mill, better known in more recent times as Billy Mill.

Henry VIII's Commissioners included Tynemouth in the second wave of the Dissolution of the Monasteries. It was surrendered on 12 January 1539 and the lands passed into private hands. In the 1630s the Percy family, Earls of Northumberland, acquired much of the inshire, and the lands around North Shields became copyhold to the Manor of Tynemouth. The East Chirton township can be equated with the village of Chirton, around Silkey's Lane and the Newcastle to Tynemouth road.

In the late seventeenth century one of the landowners was the Duke of Argyll. He had a large racing stud at Chirton Hall, where he died on 28 September 1703, allegedly after a night of debauchery in North Shields. He had passed his estate at Chirton to his companion, Mrs Allison. Despite a dispute with the family, she was able to sell the land to Robert Lawson. Local legend has it that her pet name was 'Silky', that she was murdered and that she haunted the lane which takes her name. The Lawson estate passed to Robert's cousin, Adam Cardonnel, in 1791. It is said that Mr Lawson made a detailed will, taking into consideration the descent of the land through every member of his family. On seeing the document Mr Cardonnel joked that he might as well go in at the end. The whole of the Lawson line died out and the Cardonnels inherited. They took the name de Cardonnel-Lawson.

The estate became industrialized in the nineteenth century. The Hall was demolished in 1811 with the sinking of the Burdon Main Colliery. At the riverside, Smith's Dock built a large ballast hill. The Lawsons did retain Chirton Hill Farm, part of which was taken by Preston Colliery in the 1870s. At the end of the eighteenth century the High Main coal seam was particularly prized on the London coal market. Despite constant problems with flooding, the complex of mines around Percy Main were worked until the whole of the local coalfield was drowned by 1851. In the meantime the salt industry at North Shields and Coble Dene had collapsed in 1726.

From the seventeenth century there was a growing network of wooden colliery waggonways, which were converted to iron and steel railways in the nineteenth century. On 1 June 1840 the Carrs of Seghill pit opened a railway line to Hayhole. Blyth was connected to Percy Main by a passenger line on 3 May 1847. These became the basis of the enterprising Blyth & Tyne Railway, formed in 1852, and soon to supply a new industry to Percy Main. The long fight to free the river from Newcastle ended with the creation of the Tyne Improvement Commission in 1850. One of their first acts was the conversion of the tidal Hayhole Dock. Much enlarged, it opened as the Northumberland Dock on 22 June 1857. Plans to build another basin at the Low Lights fell through, to be replaced, after much delay, by the Albert Edward Dock in 1884. To the north the Shire Moor was gradually enclosed, particularly in 1649 and 1790.

Much of the land in Middle Chirton and Balkwell was held by the Reeds. Ralph Gardner acquired the estate when he married Catherine Reed after the Civil War. He was one of the first to campaign for the emancipation of the river. At the end of the seventeenth century Chirton House was built by Winifred Milbourne. It passed to the Collingwoods, the most famous of whom was Cuthbert, Admiral Lord Collingwood, the hero of Trafalgar. He was at sea when he inherited the estate, although his wife and daughters lived there until his death.

Preston Township remained largely agricultural. Indeed, as the riverside was engulfed by heavy industry, the population came to value the district as a resort. The market gardeners in particular catered to evening and weekend walkers, providing refreshments. Much of the land south of the village was owned by branches of the Fenwick family. When the Council bought land for Preston Cemetery from John Fenwick of Preston Villa, they acknowledged the custom by laying out part of the grounds as the People's Park.

The Townships of Tynemouth, North Shields, Preston, and Chirton formed the Parliamentary Borough of Tynemouth on the Reform Act of 1832. There was already a Town Commission for North Shields, which was incorporated with the other townships as a municipal borough on 6 August 1849. It became a County Borough in 1904, and part of the Borough of North Tyneside in 1974. From an early date the local authority was interested in doing away with the run-down original settlement at North Shields. A plan to move the inhabitants to the Balk Well Farm was interrupted by the First World War. Revived in 1919, it was supplemented by the Ridges Farm housing estate in the 1930s. That was joined by the West Chirton Trading Estate, intended to replace declining heavy industry in the late 1930s. After the Second World War there was rapid expansion to the north and east of the Coast Road in the 1950s and 1960s, until much of the medieval inshire disappeared beneath suburbs of North Shields.

Pigot's Directory for 1834 stated that 'CHIRTON is a populous and straggling village, in the parish of Tynemouth, on the main road from Newcastle to North Shields, seven miles from the former and about one from the latter town. The principal support of the population of this village is derived from the collieries, which are numerous and extensive in the immediate neighbourhood. Chirton house, in this village, was the birth-place of that celebrated naval hero, the late Lord Collingwood...' Well – that last part isn't true. There is still considerable work needed to produce a comprehensive history of the villages on the outskirts of North Shields. If anyone has corrections or additions to this book, the staff of the Library would be pleased to hear from them. This introduction is necessarily a simplified account. For more extensive notes on the early history of the area the reader should consult Volume 8 of *A History of Northumberland*, being *The History of Tynemouth*, by H.H.E. Craster. Other works include *History of Shields*, by William Brockie; *England's Grievance Discovered*, by Ralph Gardner; *Making of the Tyne*, by R.W. Johnson; *Handbook to Tynemouth and Guide to the Blyth & Tyne Railway*, by Richard Welford; *Our Heritage: Preston Township and Preston Village*, by W.H. Smurthwaite; *Blyth & Tyne Railway*, by J.A. Wells. Use was also made of the *Shields Daily News* and its successors, the *Shields Hustler*, trade directories, censuses, and council minutes.

One
Dockland

The River Tyne, before 1900. The collieries of Northumberland and Durham were a major contributor to the district's economy for some 200 years. The staiths at Northumberland and Albert Edward Docks were amongst the busiest in the country.

Smith's Docks, 11 May 1951. At the south-west edge of North Shields, T. & W. Smith opened a small shipyard on the narrow strip of land below Milburn Place in 1852. It lay on the site of the sheds beside the ships. Early in the twentieth century they amalgamated with their neighbours, the Edwards' yards. By the time of this picture they were one of the largest ship-repair companies in the world. The firm's last major construction project was the building of No. 8 Dock, dug into the bank side above the Limekiln Shore from 1950. At the riverside a quay is being built to replace the last of Smith's floating docks. They had been very necessary for work on larger vessels in such limited space. The dock opened on 18 June 1954. Dock Road runs along the far edge of the excavations. The open space was once home to rows of small cottages, some of which may have been built to house the workers in the nearby collieries. Burdon Main, Chance and Hope pits flourished early in the nineteenth century.

Burdon Main Row, 10 September 1919. At one of a series of Victory Teas held during the summer, thirty-eight children were entertained, gifts were exchanged, and music played till late in a street decorated by lanterns. These houses were built at the edge of the town, along the line of a colliery waggonway.

Robson's Row, 1920s. Looking more like a typical colliery row, these cottages lay on Dock Road. In the background is the gasholder at Minton Lane.

Albert Edward Dock, 21 August 1884. The *Para e Amazonas* brought Albert Edward, Prince of Wales, to open the long awaited Coble Dene Dock. Hope House is on the bank above, with the Ballast Hill to the north.

Albert Edward Dock, 1898. Beyond the imported timber, probably from the Baltic, is the collier *France*, a steel barque, owned by Bordes et Fils. Her regular cargoes were coal from the Tyne to South America, returning with Chilean nitrates for fertilizers. She left the Tyne on 14 March 1901 for Valparaiso and disappeared in the mid-Atlantic.

Albert Edward Dock, 4 March 1905. On the previous night the recently completed No. 5 staithe caught fire. The flames spread to the extensive wood yards in a blaze seen all over Tyneside. The Ballast Hill was used to reduce the wood content in the ramp of the replacement staithe.

The grain warehouse, September 1970. The huge building seen beyond the fire wreckage, in the picture above, was constructed to encourage an expansion of imports, principally from San Francisco and the River Plate.

Albert Edward Dock, 13 September 1965. To the left of the grain store is No. 1 warehouse, used for such merchandise as mass-produced groceries. To the right is part of the Bergen Quay.

Bergen Quay, 29 June 1937. The first quay for the Bergenske Steamship Co. opened in June 1928. This is opening day for the extension and the new Custom House. The new quay was for the Oslo trade of the Fred Olsen Line. The accumulator tower used for opening the dock gates had to be moved during construction.

No. 107   Northumberland Docks, Howdon on Tyne.

Northumberland Dock, c. 1909. Hayhole Spouts were open to the river, and formed the basis of one the Tyne Commissioners' greatest works. Their river wall enclosed one of the busiest coal exporting docks in the country. It opened in 1857, and expanded wharfage was opened in 1874.

Howdon Docks. 4046

Northumberland Dock, 1910s. Each of the spouts at the ends of the staiths could load some 1,000 tons of coal per hour, serving fleets of colliers for home and foreign use.

Commissioners' Staiths. Staiths Nos 3, 4 and 5 at Whitehill Point were built before the Albert Edward Dock. Although there were ironworks along the river, the structures were principally constructed from heavy timbers.

Commissioners' Staiths. George Stephenson developed steam locomotives on the Tyneside colliery railways. Nonetheless, gravity, static winding engines, and even horses continued to provide motive power well into the nineteenth century.

Minnie Beck's, c. 1970. The Dock Hotel was in one family from the 1870s, at first the Gibsons, then the Becks. Mary Ann Gillinder, née Minnie Beck, was supposed to be a teetotaller. It was known that she would refuse to serve anyone she took against, and would close rather than tolerate rowdiness. At the age of eighty-six, in July 1973, she was savagely attacked. The house never re-opened, and was demolished in 1974. The redoubtable landlady died in December 1976.

Overleaf: Northumberland Dock. The Duke of Northumberland's Hayhole Dock lay on the site of Associated Lead, a factory considerably expanded in 1970. Although only a tidal pool, Hayhole exported 1 million tons of coal. It was partly to protect this trade that the Tyne Improvement Commission built the original 55-acre dock. The basin eventually extended from Percy Bank to East Howdon, the community seen to the left. Above is the old colliery and railway village of Percy Main, with the Meadow Well estate to the right. There are remnants of extensive sidings on both sides of the Esso oil tanks, which first came on line in 1960. At the riverside are the old locks, below the dock offices. With the coal export trade declining and ships growing, the dock was declared obsolete. Early in 1958 a large section of river wall had been breached, and the much of the dock was filled to provide standing for the Danish container traffic.

Northumberland Dock, 2 May 1930. Amongst a cluster of industrial buildings was one of James Georgeson's shops. He had others at Burdon Main Row and on the outskirts of North Shields, at Queen Alexandra Road, between 1920 and 1951.

Dock offices, 1880s.

Flatworth Mill, 1890s. Tynemouth Priory had a mill at Flatworth in the twelfth century. The tower stood at the west side of the Albert Edward Dock. Alexander Russell was the miller in the 1820s. He died in 1858, and the mill may have been converted to housing shortly thereafter.

Pheasant Cottage, *c.* 1930. In the mid-nineteenth century this was a market gardener's cottage on the edge of Chirton Dene, home to the Johnson family. By the time of the picture the dene, in the foreground, was being filled, and the area was enclosed by timber yards. On the steps are Ald Porter and his daughter-in-law.

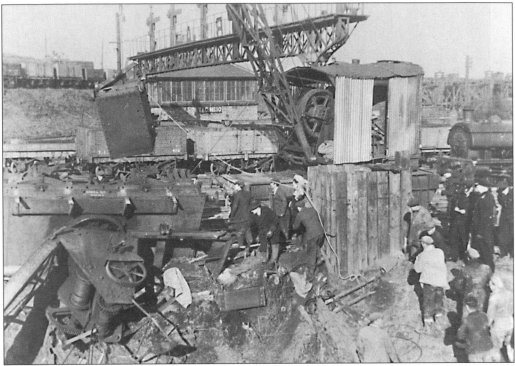

Tyne Improvement Commissioners yards, 4 April 1951. A crane was being used to build a drain when it toppled into the trench. One of the operators was killed. Another crane is being used to dismantle the boiler.

Northumberland Dock, 1932. At the left is 'Big Jim Ridley' of Tynemouth Electricity Department. The men are installing the 6,000-volt cable for the new Howdon Staithe, at the west end of the dock. It opened on 16 December 1932, serving Hartley Main collieries.

Easton & Gallant Terraces, East Howdon-on-Tyne. 1044

East Howdon, *c.* 1910. S. Easten applied for permission to build eighty houses in February 1899; and G.J. Gallant's further application was approved in the December. The first residents on each estate who have been traced in electoral rolls appeared in 1905 and 1901 respectively.

East Howdon war memorial, 1919. The names on the poster are illegible, but some local men can be traced. J.U. Lillie went down with the *Earl of Elgin*; R. Roland and F. McVay died in action with the Northumberland Fusiliers; J. Shea was killed in France in the Royal Naval Division; Francis Smith was lost with the *Defence* at Jutland. William Miller is in the middle row, third from the left.

East Howdon-on-Tyne. 4043

East Howdon, *c.* 1910. In 1921 Tynemouth Council took the open space in front of Telford street, to the left, and built blocks of flats. They were completed by July 1922, and named Frater Terrace. Baird Terrace was built at the same time.

TO ALBERT EDWARD DOCK
AND COAL STAITHS

TYNE COMMISSION QUA

Howdon Road, 1 May 1931. Trams ran along the road from East Howdon to North Shields between 1902 and 1930. Percy Main lies off camera to the left, and the Minton Lane gasworks is in the distance.

Two
Percy Main

High Row, 1890s. The cottages were built parallel to the Backworth Colliery Railway. The inhabitants have gathered for some special occasion in the lane at the back. Beyond is the embankment for the North Eastern Railway between Newcastle and North Shields.

Percy Main, *c.* 1900. In the doorway to the right is Mrs Elizabeth Miller, *née* Johnson (1860-1927). Beside her is her grandson, Joseph, and in the other door is her daughter Marcy. The 'city of the seven lamps' took its name from the valuable High Main coal seam, the rights to which were held by the Percy family, the Dukes of Northumberland. Work began in 1799, converting a largely rural area to industry, and forcing the demolition of Lawson's Hall. The workings extended under the village, and continued as far as Howdon Pans, where shrinkage caused considerable problems. All the local collieries were flooded out by 1851, following the breakdown of a joint pumping agreement. Although the Old Pit, to the east, was revived, mining ceased in the village. However, Percy Main lay between the inland collieries and the riverside staiths, and became the focus of many of the waggonways. From 1847, at the height of the railway boom, a number of the private lines began to come together as the Blyth & Tyne Railway Company. Royal Assent to the Bill to create the company was given in 1852. The village became the headquarters of this small but vigorous enterprise, and for a century railways were a major employer.

Middle Row, *c.* 1900. Another picture of Mrs Miller, this time with her sister, Jenny Johnson.

Mrs Hannah Mary Thompson, *née* Skipsey, at No. 19 Low Row in the 1890s.

St James' Terrace, 24 November 1949. The colliery which gave the village its name was long gone, but still made its presence felt. The large areas of re-pointing are due to mining subsidence.

St James' Terrace, 7 March 1958. Despite some rebuilding, the house continued to suffer problems.

Percy Main Cricket Club, 1969. There are records suggesting clubs were set up in the village in around 1861 and 1872. Another was formed about 1885. The ground east of St John's church was taken in 1905.

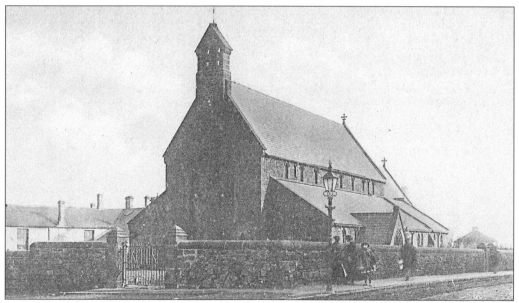

St John's church, c. 1900. In 1860 it was decided to divide the Parish of Tynemouth. The Duke of Northumberland agreed to fund the building of the new churches. St John's was consecrated in September 1864.

St John's Terrace, *c.* 1910. In the distance is the spire above the Percy Main Council School.

St John's Terrace, *c.* 1910. Although Dr Weidner's name is over the door, Dr Babst's plate is still on the railings. Dr Babst had his surgery here between 1894 and 1907. Dr Weidner took over at Percy Main about 1909. He had a keen interest in the village cricket and football clubs.

Council School, Percy Main.

The Council School, c. 1905. Following the 1870 Education Act a School Board was elected for the Borough of Tynemouth. Since there was already a National School at Percy Main, a Board School at the village was not felt to be a priority. The inhabitants did vote for a new school eventually; it opened on 1 February 1892. At first, education to Standards I and II only was offered, increased to Standard V from May 1893. The infants' school, to the left, opened in September 1900. It was the last constructed by the Tynemouth School Board, before its powers passed to the local authority in 1902. The school at the corner of St John's Terrace and Nelson Terrace was replaced on 28 January 1968 by new buildings closer to Howdon Road. The foundation stone for the Anglican National School, St John's, was laid on 14 September 1869, on the north side of St John's church. It was spirited resistance from the supporters of a spiritual element in education that delayed the development of the Board School. A new building was erected in 1975, but in 1998 falling school rolls led the governors to opt for closure.

Percy Main Council School, 1951. Miss I.M. McAllister is seen with a group which includes Jean Cockburn, Alma Fuge, Ann Laidler, Margaret McCall, Noreen Mavin, Helen Mays, Dorothy Newman, Ellen Parker, Margaret Robinson, Margaret Thompson, Margaret Waterworth and Ann Wood.

Percy St John's Junior School, 1948. Standing to the right is the headmaster, Mr Home. On the back row, second from the left, is Albert Bishop.

Percy Main Council School, 24 May 1921. Under instruction of the Education Committee, the school celebrated Empire Day. The local newspaper reported that the children spent the morning singing patriotic songs, dressed in traditional costumes of the Empire.

Percy Main School football team, 1920. From left to right, back row: D. Robertson, J. Hull, B. Abernathy, Mr Cockburn, H. Knott, J. Usher, W. Rennie. Middle row: Mr Fairy, E. Little, C. Miller, D. Rutherford, S. Rutherford, J. Kerr, E. Page. Front row: S. Alexander, J. Harrison, J. Little, J. Dugdale. Three boys are wearing County caps. The team played eighteen matches in the Tynemouth Schools League in 1920, winning seventeen and drawing one.

Engine sheds, August 1969. Colliery waggonways clustered around Percy Main as early as the 1780s. The Blyth & Tyne Railway company began work on building engine sheds and workshops at Percy Main in 1854. The works were vital to local lines and the village economy under the North Eastern Railway and British Railways up to the 1960s.

British Railways Staff Association hut, October 1958. 'The Hut' was kept on sufferance, until more commodious premises opened in October 1961.

A brake van of unknown date. Jumping aboard railway wagons was regarded as legitimate transport, and a popular game. The results were sometimes fatal.

A.R. Emmerson & Co., 1950s. Adam Rutherford Emmerson was a grocer and postmaster in Burdon Street before setting up as a carter. He died in 1955, but the business continued until 1977. Second from the left is Bob Higgins, then Billy Emmerson, Peter Emmerson, Walter Savoury and Jimmy Emmerson.

Burdon Street, *c.* 1910. Looking north towards the railway station, the pinnacles of the Primitive Methodist church are seen to the left. Much of this part of the village disappeared in the mid-1970s.

The Primitive Methodist church, *c.* 1902. The 'Ranters' had a presence in the village in the 1820s. They began a Sunday school in 1884 and their services were held there until this church opened on 22 March 1902.

The post office, 1940s. Percy Dagg was a pharmacist in Burdon Street from the early 1920s.

Martha Meldram, c. 1890. The original carte de visite was inscribed 'Postmistress, Percy Main'. Mrs Meldram can be traced as the sub-postmistress from 1859 to 1879. She seems to have taken the post following the loss at sea of her husband, Captain George Meldram. She died in 1891.

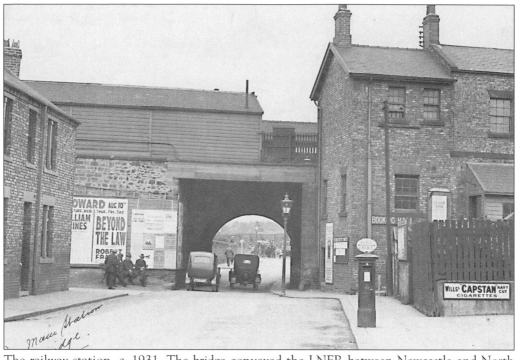

The railway station, *c.* 1931. The bridge conveyed the LNER between Newcastle and North Shields. In the background are wagon sets on one of the colliery lines.

Railway bridge, 16 April 1936. Workmen on the north side of the bridge are breaking a pedestrian tunnel beneath the station, to the left of the arch in the picture above.

The railway station, *c.* 1905. The Newcastle & North Shields Railway was the first purpose-built passenger line on Tyneside. It opened in 1839. Under the North Eastern Railway it became part of the Tyneside loop line, and these electric trains began running in 1904.

Percy Main, No. Shields

The Percy Arms, *c.* 1905. Seen from the station, the Seaton Burn Colliery Waggonway runs past the pub. Beyond is the Backworth Colliery line. High Row is in the distance, and the roof of St John's vicarage is just visible above the trees.

"Vicarage", Percy Main, No: Shields.

The vicarage, c. 1920. From the road over the colliery railways the photographer looked down on the junction of Wallsend Road, to the left, and Waterville Road, to the right. Between them are the grounds of the Percy Main vicarage.

Redburn public house, 1959. Previously St John's vicarage, the pub opened on 18 December 1956. After thirty-five years' residence, the Revd John Clucas was reported as being uneasy at the transformation.

Mindrum Terrace, c. 1905. At a ceremony in October 1943 the members of Percy Main Social Club took possession of their premises after forty years. Surviving founders were G. Couchman, R. Coulthard, P. Emmerson, J. Peart, S. Morton, E. Strathearn, J. Thirlwell and A. Hepple.

Percy Main Social Club, 1959. A.W. McDonald of the CWS Bank arranged a loan necessary for an extension, and helped save the club when it was in danger of closing in 1932. After a period of prosperity, which saw a new building on Norham Road, the club went into receivership in 1987.

Redburn View, 1 October 1958. Multi-storey flats were a popular solution to the need for social housing, and Tynemouth councillors were impressed by those they saw at Fawdon. Work started on eighteen five-storey blocks in the spring of 1957. These were built along the line of the Red Burn, running down to the Coble Dene on land that had long been used for tipping, and was underlain by coal workings. They soon fell out of favour, and most of the blocks to the north were demolished. Those to the south were extensively refurbished.

Previous page: Percy Main, 1958. Percy Main station is at the bottom, with part of Redburn View at Hunter's Close in the middle. To the left is the Redburn pub at the foot of Norham Road. The white building along Wallsend Road is the Pineapple Inn. Opposite is St Joseph's Roman Catholic church, opened in August 1955. The land had been Ord's market garden.

Three
Meadow Well

Waterville Road, 10 December 1934. The Ridges estate is growing west from North Shields. In the distance is the Meadow Well farmhouse.

Meadow Well Farm, 1890s. Meadow Well Cottage took its name from an excellent spring. It had been an inn, but lost the licence in the mid-nineteenth century. Later it was run by the Hewitt family as a dairy farm. Following a transfer of the licence from the Wheatsheaf, the Ridges Inn was built on part of the site; it was later the Seine Boat. The 1930 Housing Act encouraged Tynemouth Corporation to return to a long held ambition to demolish the slums of the bankside town. Plans for 850 houses were drawn up in November 1930. In February 1931 the Duke of Northumberland's agent offered 135 acres west of the town, and the council eventually agreed to take $132\frac{1}{2}$ acres for £24,000. Rents were fixed at 6s 6d for a three-bedroomed house, 7s 1d for four, and 7s 10d for five. There were two farms – the Meadow Well and the Ridges. The tenants of the latter were given notice to quit, and on 9 January 1933 it was decreed that it would give its name to the new estate. At the time J.W. Black, editor of the *Shields Hustler*, declared that it would have been better to call it after the former. After revitalization in 1969 the Council did change the name, and in 1972 many of the street names were altered.

Linden Road, 18 September 1934. The road ran down from the Ridges farmstead. Barrow & Co. were the contractors. The street name later became Lowdham Avenue.

Linden Road, 6 September 1935. The same road is seen from the south. Most of this part of the estate had tree names, such as Firtree, Cherrywood, and Briarwood.

Marina Avenue, *c.* 1959. James Drury was a grocer at Marina Avenue from the 1940s. The road was later renamed Avon Avenue.

Marina Avenue, *c.* 1959. Beyond the Meadow Well chip shop is H. Newham's general dealership.

Marina Avenue, c. 1959. To the right are the premises of J.H. Potts (North Shields) Ltd. The tobacconist and confectioner's company was registered by James H. Potts in 1959, to take over the existing business.

Marina Avenue, c. 1960. Gibson's shop adjoined that of J.H. Potts. Next door is John Day's greengrocery. A branch library was mooted in 1947, and in 1949 the Housing Committee agreed to build one with flats above. It opened on 14 October 1952.

The library in 1976. In an effort to make the branch more popular, the library was relaunched as the Meadowell Book Centre. The stock and surroundings were intended to appear as informal as possible. In the background are staff members Winnie Little and Brian West.

Marina Avenue, c. 1959. James Dunn had a butcher's shop in Milburn Place, before the slum clearances, and he followed his customers out of the town. Ina Watson's business used to be in Church Street before the Second World War.

Woodlea Square, 16 October 1936. The council opted to provide housing specially designed for the elderly, with a square of single-storey accommodation, intended to be in a more peaceful part of the estate.

Square Housing Trust, 1930s. In March 1929 a meeting of the Northumberland Square Presbyterian church was prompted to form a housing trust, to provide the lowest possible rents. The first houses opened before the end of the year. More were begun and by 1937 forty-eight homes had been completed on Howdon Road, to the south of the Ridges estate.

Rose Cottage, 2 September 1941. This small shop on Waterville Road had suffered from bomb blast.

Neville Engineering Co. Ltd, April 1958. The garage firm on Waterville Road was registered as a limited company in November 1962. The directors were Neville M. and Dorothy Wilkie of Tynemouth.

Monk & Co., April 1958. Gordon C.
Monk started with one lorry in 1946
and built up a flourishing garage
business. A Londoner, he came to
North Shields on leaving the Royal
Marines. He died in 1970. In the
background is the chimney of the
gasworks.

The gasworks, 29 October 1971.
Number 2 retort house, built at the
beginning of the twentieth century, is
undergoing demolition.

The gasworks, *c*. 1934. The first North Shields gasworks was built at the Low Lights in 1819. The company was re-organized in the 1860s and the directors became concerned that the site was restrictive. They took the opportunity to acquire land between Meadowell, or Minton, Lane and the railway. A new works opened toward the end of 1871. Full-time production ceased in 1930.

Silkey's Lane, 18 September 1934. To the north is Chirton Front Street, seen from Waterville Road. In the distance are Chirton Club and the Co-operative bakery. The spire at Chirton School is just visible on the horizon.

Four
Chirton and Balkwell

Chirton House, August 1900. The mansion was rebuilt in 1693 by Winifred Milbourne. In later years it was home to her relations the Collingwoods and the Reeds. William Horsley bought the house in 1876. It was demolished in 1901 to make way for a Co-operative Society bakery.

Chirton Cottage, late seventeenth century. Ralph Gardner was born in Newcastle, but moved to the cottage at Chirton Green in the 1640s, on marrying Catherine Reed, the widow of a local landowner. He fell foul of the vested interests of traders in Newcastle when he opened a brewery, and was imprisoned for trading outside the city. In 1655 he published a petition addressed to Oliver Cromwell, entitled *England's Grievance Discovered*, laying out centuries of restrictions placed on the trade of the Tyne. The matter went to Parliament, and local people hoped that North Shields would become a market town. However Parliament was dissolved the day before a decision was due. There is no record of what became of Ralph Gardner. His house was replaced by Chirton Cottage in around 1856. From the 1860s to 1917 it was the home of John Foster Spence, once an active campaigner for the Tyne Improvement Commission. When John Robert Hogg's widow died in 1940, the land was offered to the council. The cottage was pulled down in 1948, during an expansion of Ralph Gardner School. Chirton House is in the background. Soon after its construction Miss Milbourne married John Roddam. A daughter, Mary, married Edward Collingwood of Byker, and his son passed the estate to his cousin, Cuthbert Collingwood. For his part in the Battle of Trafalgar, Admiral Collingwood was raised to the peerage. Lady Collingwood lived there between 1806 and 1810. On Lord Collingwood's death in that year, the house passed to his brother. His nephew, Edward John Collingwood, left the area in 1841, passing the house to his brother-in-law, the Revd Christopher Reed, Vicar of Tynemouth.

Chirton Cottage, *c.* 1900. The house was the first home of Great Northern Knitwear, before they moved to the West Chirton Estate.

Frederick Taylor, *c.* 1910. Mr Taylor was a gardener at Chirton Cottage. As a practical joke he hid a note on the premises, purporting to be a reference to a treasure secreted by Ralph Gardner in 1653. Years later there was considerable excitement when it came to light during the demolition. The council called on the Public Record Office for a report.

Chirton Green, *c.* 1910. Following an appeal for public subscriptions by Borough Treasurer T.T. Clark, Shotton Bros built the Ralph Gardner memorial to a design by Gilbert Park. It was erected in 1882.

Horsley's Cottages, 1889. The original picture is inscribed 'Doggy Nanny's Cottage'. The more formal name was used when the picture was reprinted in the *Shields Daily News* in 1939. The cottages were on the edge of Chirton Green.

Chirton service station, 7 September 1960. John Hewitt had recently opened his garage at the corner of Front Street and Silkey's Lane, on the site of the Co-operative bakery. Five years later his wife opened another, opposite.

Chirton Junior School, 16 April 1941. Blast damage forced the pupils to use Queen Victoria School until Collingwood School opened in September 1951. In the background is the wreckage of the Rex Cinema.

Collingwood Junior School staff, 1957. From left to right, back row: Moira Wilson, -?-, Pat Armstrong, Jim Nicholson, Jack Hewetson, ? Hardy, Ken Graham, -?-, Rita Axelson, Miss Popplewell. Seated third from the left is Miss Goldsack. Mr Dobson and Mr Hipkin are in the middle, with Joyce Mewes and Audrey Hipgrave at the end.

Billy Mill Lane, 16 April 1941. The bomb at Chirton School severely damaged surrounding houses. Misses E.M. Townsley and A. Nicholson were commended for their aid to neighbouring houses.

Billy Mill Lane, 1924. This small enclosure contained Jewish burials from the early nineteenth century. In order to widen the road near the corner of the Quadrant, the Jewish authorities granted permission for the remains to be transferred to Preston Cemetery.

Chirton Hill Farm, c. 1905. The house stood on Billy Mill Lane, near the site of the junction with Addington Crescent. In the distance, to the north, are the workings at Ritson's Preston Colliery.

The Balkwell, North Shields. 5688

The Quadrant, *c.* 1920. In May 1922 the council opted to rename Number 3 to Number 10 Streets on the Balkwell Estate. They were respectively Oswin Terrace, Sunniside, Burt Avenue, Eustace Avenue, Delaval Avenue, The Quadrant, Ogle Terrace and Balkwell Avenue. New Road became Chirton Green.

Previous page: Balkwell in the 1950s. The stand of trees to the left was all that was left of the plantation around West Chirton Hall. It became part of the Norham High School site, opened in 1973 to replace the Municipal High School. Wallsend Road runs along the bottom of the frame, up to the junction with Balkwell Avenue, which cuts across the middle towards the top left, passing the site of the Balk Well Farm. Near the centre are the white roofs of Collingwood School, with Verne Road just beyond. Parallel to it is the Coast Road, just below Billy Mill and the quarries. To the left the curve of the Quadrant leads round to Addington Crescent. Beyond the Coast Road are Lynn Road and Preston Cemetery.

Robert Westall, *c.* 1947. A resident at 18 Balkwell Green through most of the 1930s and 1940s, Robert Westall in later years used his experiences of growing up on Tyneside to write a number of prize-winning books. He died in 1993.

Pineapple Inn, *c.* 1959. On 9 December 1787 a son was born to John Dobson, publican and gardener. Young John became famous for his designs for the centre of Newcastle, and for country mansions. Outside this pub in 1832 a group of miners, armed and sworn as constables, shot dead Cuthbert Skipsey, father of Joseph Skipsey, the pitman poet of Percy Main.

Wallsend Road, *c.* 1959. Florence Woodhead established a confectioner's shop in the 1930s, seen to the left as J.A. Woodhead. At the time C.E. Willets' boot repair business was round the corner in Cartington Road. Alex Baird replaced C.O. Lawrence as the chemist.

Wallsend Road, *c.* 1959. In the 1930s Robert English had 120 Wallsend Road as a dairyman. Next door was Margaret Fisher, radio dealer and grocer. Shortly before the Second World War she was replaced by Ada V. Winter.

Verne Road, 12 January 1934. The shopping centre was to be called Main Street, but residents objected, so in December 1931 it became Verne Road. To the left are Mrs Jane E. Jones, general dealer, and William F. Irvin's Balkwell Fruit Store. The Accumulator Charging Services are on the far side of Heaton Terrace, and Billy Mill Lane is in the distance.

Verne Road, c. 1959. J. & S. Irwin have replaced Mrs Jones, and a branch of Carrick's bakery is where R.H. Knott, confectioner, had been.

Verne Road, *c.* 1959. George Costigan had the chemist's shop on the corner of Heaton Terrace for eighteen years, until his death in 1966.

Verne Road, *c.* 1959. John Usher was a prominent newsagent and active in the Chamber of Trade. In 1959 he became a councillor at his first attempt. The Heaton Road branch of the North Shields Co-operative Society was part of their post-war drive to expand.

Cartington Road, 10 April 1941. Arthur Thompson's fishmonger's shop in West Percy Street was destroyed in the same air raid that killed him at Cartington Road. He had been world junior weightlifting champion.

Heaton Terrace, 5 May 1941. Seven members of the Docherty family, of 132 Heaton Terrace, were dug out of their Anderson shelter alive.

A ward in the smallpox hospital, *c.* 1923. An outbreak of smallpox at the beginning of the year found the borough short of hospital beds. Some patients had to be sent out of the area. A separate smallpox unit was built at the north-west of the Balkwell Estate, to replace the ward at Moor Park hospital which had to be burnt down before ordinary cases of scarlet fever and diphtheria could be admitted. In 1938 the Borough Surveyor recommended removing the smallpox hospital for the development of the Balkwell and West Chirton Estates.

The administration block of the smallpox hospital, *c.* 1923.

High Flatworth Farm, 18 April 1949. From the 1860s the farm was tenanted by the Johnson family, during which time there was a Dun Cow pub behind the barn. About the time the Meikles took over, in the 1890s, the pub closed. The Nicholson family held the farm from the 1920s until the Second World War, followed by a number of short term tenants. The last farmer was Alfred Elwen. When he moved in, in March 1962, his landlord, the Duke of Northumberland, approached the council for help in installing electricity – the farm still used oil lamps. The council had been considering converting the 22-acre farm to industrial land since 1955. Shortly after an inspection by the President of the Board of Trade in 1965, the farm became part of the West Chirton Trading Estate. At one point in the 1930s Tynemouth had a higher percentage of unemployed than Jarrow. The council decided the area needed new industries. Around 1938 they acquired 52 acres of West Chirton Farm, on Balkwell Lane, and in a local Act incorporated powers to build a trading estate and houses for the workers. The borough had Special Area status, enabling Great Northern Knitwear to move into a new factory early in 1938. The West Chirton Trading Estate was officially opened in October 1938, at which time sweet manufacturers Welch & Sons were building a factory on Norham Road. The war delayed further development, although the council was actively promoting the estate from 1942. A huge Ministry of Supply depot, built in 1945, provided ready-made buildings for post-war use.

Norham Road, c. 1960. In the centre is the Tynemouth bus depot, with Great Northern Knitwear to the right. Next door are Clay & Sons, clothing manufacturers. They arrived from Luton in 1943, looking for a reliable workforce. Joblings Glassware and High Flatworth Farm are in the background.

Tynemouth bus depot, c. 1959. The Tynemouth name was used for service buses and the coaches took Thomas Wakefield's name, from the charabanc fleet bought in 1929.

Norham Road, c. 1960. The building with white markings on the roof will be remembered as North Tyneside Bakeries. Opposite the side road is the Ronson factory, with the Hall Sections engineering site next door. Welch's sweet factory is towards the top right.

Welch & Sons Ltd, c. 1959. The firm was founded by Thomas L. Welch, who died in 1967. Always popular in the North East, at one time they also exported a significant percentage of their production.

Norham Road, *c.* 1960. In the centre are the Ministry of Supply sheds, which began to close in 1948. Tyne Furniture Works had already moved onto the site next to the Coast Road, on the right, and Malone Instruments went into the sheds.

De La Rue Insulation Ltd, *c.* 1960. The factory opened without ceremony in 1947, and Formica production began in 1948. A million-pound melamine chipboard plant opened in 1974. In November 1976 they merged with Arborite, on the opposite side of the Coast Road.

Five
Billy Mill and the Shire Moor

Billy Mill, c. 1895. The ruined windmill, seen from the old quarry. Unlike other mills in the area, Billy Mill was never converted to a residence, but it did see service as a Scout hut, and as a Home Guard observation post.

Billy Mill, 1951. The small community is shown here in a view to the north, from the Coast Road. The old Cannon Inn is hidden by the buildings to the left. A Billing's Mill can be traced in the fourteenth-century records of Tynemouth Priory, and a new stob-mill was built in the 1590s. In 1658 the neighbouring quarry was in the hands of Ralph Gardner, whose encroachments were described as threatening the mill. It was still in position in 1722, but burned shortly afterwards. The stone tower was constructed in 1760. However, the advent of steam mills at Chirton and Willington Quay rendered Billy Mill redundant. In 1964 Tynemouth Council refused permission to build three-storey flats on the site, and decided to protect the remains. When S. Storer & Son received permission to build eight houses, the council sought the advice of Tynemouth Civic Society. It was reported that in their opinion it was a 'cylindrical hulk of industrial masonry from a past era', of sentimental value only. Sentiment was not allowed to hold sway, and the ruins came down in September 1967. The quarry was owned by the Robson brothers in the early nineteenth century, and later by Shotton Bros. Both used the stone for many buildings in North Shields. About 1890 the quarry was taken by Hutchinson & Son. The original works became a rifle range, and production continued at Moor Houses.

The Coast Road at Billy Mill, North Shields.   8779

Coast Road, *c.* 1930. The Coast Road was opened on 27 October 1927, to provide a fast route from Newcastle. Rapidly growing traffic led to a call to widen the highway in 1939, but the war put an end the plans. They were revived in 1948.

Cannon Inn, 15 January 1959. The licence of the council-owned Cannon Inn, opposite Billy Mill, was transferred in 1934, to allow the construction of this new building. It was built between the remnant of an old lane, seen above, and the Coast Road.

Billy Mill, Lynn Road and Chirton Grange estates, 30 March 1954.

Coast Road, 1950. The view is northwards, along Norham Road North towards Moor Park. The original Coast Road was already too narrow for the growing volume of traffic.

Coast Road, c. 1964. On 28 November 1963 the first sod was cut for the Tynemouth Borough section of the Coast Road duplication scheme. It was opened by Dame Irene Ward in December 1964, a year early.

Coast Road, *c.* 1960. October 1960 saw the beginning of work to extend the road down to the seafront at Tynemouth. At the junction of Queen Alexandra Road West and Billy Mill Lane is the Preston Colliery memorial, later moved into Preston Cemetery. The extension was fully opened in November 1961.

Collingwood Garage, *c.* 1960. The garage between Lynn Road and Queen Alexandra Road West had to be demolished in sections to allow through the Beach Road extension of the Coast Road. New premises were built behind.

Chirton Grange Estate. In June 1950 Tynemouth Council decided to buy 40 acres of land between Whitehouse Lane and Rake Lane. Preston White House is to the right, Chirton Grange Farm is at the top left, and Rake Lane is at the top.

White House Farm, 3 July 1951. Much of Tynemouth Shire Moor was enclosed in 1649, and five farms were created. During the nineteenth century Preston White House was tenanted by the Potts and Dunn families. It was held by Mr Close when the new estate was begun.

Moor Houses, c. 1958. St Anselm's Roman Catholic High School is under construction on the line of the old lane to Billy Mill. First planned as Lynn Road Secondary Modern, it became St Cuthbert's in 1954. Work began in 1956, and it opened on 5 January 1959 as St Anselm's. It became St Thomas More School in 1988. Part of the Lynn Road estate is at the bottom right. The cluster of sheds and vehicles is in Mitchison's Quarry. Moor Park Hospital is to the top left. This was a fairly remote spot in January 1902, when some of the crew of the ship *Jacoma* arrived from Blyth, carrying smallpox. Within weeks eighty-three people were infected. Schools were closed until June, the clothing and bedding of possible contacts were disinfected or burned, and wallpaper was stripped from their homes. There was much lime-washing of confined spaces, and fire engines hosed down the streets. The Percy Square isolation hospital and the Port of Tyne floating hospital were quickly overwhelmed. In March 1902 the council voted to buy 5 acres of North Balkwell Farm, on which to erect prefabricated cottages as Moor Park Isolation Hospital. After the epidemic it was decided to retain Moor Park for the treatment of three diseases that were then legally notifiable: scarlet fever, diphtheria, and enteric fever. Twenty years later there were twenty-one such diseases. A number of alterations and extensions were carried out from 1930, including a new tuberculosis pavilion and an administration block. Electricity was installed in 1931. Moor Park closed as a geriatric hospital in 1986.

A Wallis & Steevens traction engine, *c.* 1910. Hutchinson & Son of Tynemouth used the tractor for cartage when they owned the Billy Mill quarry, between 1890 and the 1920s.

Mitchison's Quarry, 11 October 1956. Trees and the hospital conceal the factories on Norham Road North.

Moor Park Hospital, 24 March 1939. Scarlet fever and diphtheria were once normal childhood hazards and many people around North Shields spent part of their youth in these cottages, seeing their parents only at a distance.

Moor Park Hospital, 1935. The Medical Officer of Health urgently requested an administration block and nurses' home for a number of years. It was opened on 5 November 1935.

Norham Road North, 10 April 1948. North Eastern Trading Estates provided sites for British Diecasting, to the left, and Dukes & Marcus beyond. Bombed out of their London home, they brought their Dumarsel House clothing business via Kendal and Hotspur Hall, Whitley Bay. North Balkwell Farm is in the background, Darras Drive at the bottom, and Woolsington Road to the right.

Darras Drive, May 1948.

New York Village, *c.* 1950, looking west to the Allotments and Backworth.

Wheatsheaf Inn, *c.* 1900. The Logan family can be traced in the Backworth area in the 1860s. Three of the brothers bought land at New York in 1878, and about that time one of them, Walter, took the Wheatsheaf, on the outskirts of the village. He died there in 1907.

Dun Cow Inn, New York, *c.* 1910. The name can be traced in directories back to 1847, and in 1828 there was a Red Cow in the area. The original Dun Cow, however, was set further back on this site. About this time it was run by the Currells, who were also local farmers.

New York Road, 3 November 1954. William Thompson moved to New York from Preston, where he ran a chip shop (see p. 105). The picture was taken for one of a number of council surveys to locate unsightly advertisements.

Murton School, 1937. Murton School Board was elected in November 1874. They built a school in New York, which was enlarged in 1888 and 1906. Here Miss Sadler is seen with some of the girls at the Seaton School Holiday Camp. The school celebrated its centenary in 1978, but closed in 1991, and the land was cleared for housing.

Murton House Farm, July 1969. Known as 'Jackson's Farm' since Robert Henry Jackson arrived in the 1920s, it had been Murton House since at least the 1820s, when it was held by W. Collingwood. He was followed by Edward Collingwood, the Hansells, Reeds and Stothards.

Rake Lane drift, July 1951. Huge opencast workings grew either side of Rake Lane from 16 February 1948. Restoration had begun by 1949, but in June 1951 a deep drift mine was proposed. The pit heap is seen from the back of Murton House Farm.

Six
Preston Township

Preston Colliery, *c.* 1920. Wallace the pony was fifteen years old at this date and had spent ten years underground. The horse holder seems dressed in his best; the man to the left is in working dress.

Preston Colliery, 1921. The mine owners decided to terminate the miners' contracts and reduce pay. After negotiations failed, a lockout was declared on 31 March, and a strike on 12 April dragged on until July. Preston Colliery recorded those colliery officials who remained at their posts to maintain the pit. From left to right, back row: M. Whitehead, S. Garfitt, ? Dunn, R. Harrison, T. Wilson, -?-, -?-, -?-, -?-. Third row: G. Skelton, -?-, -?-, Browell, D. Graham, -?-, -?-, -?-, ? Harrison. Second row: ? Younger, -?-, ? Errington, -?-, A. Hall, J. Errington, Thewlis, -?-, -?-, W.J. Adams, -?-, -?-. Front row: Mr Summerbell (manager), -?-, -?-, A. Summerbell, J. Townsley, -?-, Bill Mountry, F. Summerbell, S. Ellis, W. Charlton, -?-, ? Watson, ? Thompson, Bill Knox. Thomas Hughes of Hylton Lodge began a mine on the site of Appleby Park, which won coal at the end of 1856. It also became part of North Shields' water supply. In the 1860s the pit was worked by Johnson & Osbeck. It was presumably they who sank the new shaft on Billy Mill Lane, around 1872. The Hawkey's Lane mine fell into ruin, although still used by the water company. In the mid-1870s John Shimmen was listed as the coal-owner, but by 1879 it was Robert Lindsey Hutchinson. The company built its first rail link around 1897. In the spring of 1899 Preston Colliery was sold to U.A. Ritson & Co. The chairman, J.B. van Heck, named a new shaft after his fiancée, Edwina Burr Ewing, in 1900. Attempts to find new seams failed and the pit closed in October 1928, throwing over 1,000 miners out of work. Although not as disaster-prone as some pits, Preston did have an explosion in November 1900. Samuel Mordue, Francis Dunn, John Foster Cole, Frank S. Martin and Mr Killen died; seven others were injured. A memorial was erected on Billy Mill Lane in 1902.

Preston Colliery, 1921. Greybird, Logan, Peacock and Blackbird won the Palmer Challenge Cup at the Northumberland Show. A special prize went to the oldest pony, Nick, on the right. He was still sound at the age of twenty-three, after eighteen years of work.

Tudor Avenue, 5 February 1948. In 1930 a firelighter works opened in the colliery yard. The larger building to the right was the old power house. Through the 1950s it was home to Stella Building Products, makers of wood wool slabs (reconstituted wood pressed into blocks and used for construction). They moved to a new factory in 1957 and the colliery site was cleared in 1958.

Hawkey's Lane, *c*. 1930. The large building at the bottom right was built as the Preston Miners' Hall in the 1890s. From 1919 it was Smith's Docks apprentices' hall, and later a boys' club. Next door was the council's salt water reservoir, used for flushing the sewers. From 1907 it was used to teach children to swim, under the auspices of the Tynemouth Amateur Swimming Club. To the centre and right is the Tynemouth Victoria Jubilee Infirmary. In 1875 L.H. Leslie set up the Flower Mission to take posies and Bible readings to the sick poor. They began to lend sickroom equipment in 1877 and appointed a nurse in 1880. At that time the only hospital services in the area were provided by the Workhouse sick ward; serious cases were sent to Newcastle. A small infirmary opened at Dockwray Square in August 1884. Shortly afterwards the Duke of Northumberland gave a site for a hospital in Hawkey's Lane. The foundation stone was laid in 1887, and the Victoria Jubilee Infirmary was opened on 3 August 1889. It was built on the section to the right next to the trees. A public meeting in February 1919 resolved that the borough war memorial would take the form of an extension to the Infirmary. The official opening was held in 1925, although the pavilion wards were yet to be built. The hospital operated as a charity until the advent of the National Health Service.

Hawkey's Lane Baths, c. 1910. For some thirty years J.W. Moore attended at Tynemouth Haven as swimming master of the Amateur Swimming Club. They approached the Council for permission to use the salt water reservoir, and the results were so impressive that a formal swimming pool was built.

WAR MEMORIAL AND INFIRMARY, NORTH SHIELDS.

War memorial, c. 1930. The infirmary extension to the left was the official borough memorial. During construction there was considerable local controversy over the design, or need, for the memorial plaque to the right.

Tynemouth Victoria Jubilee Infirmary, 1919. The nurses are standing on the steps of the Victorian part of the building.

The Primitive Methodist church, 25 February 1955. The North Shields Circuit sold their chapel on Saville Street to Woolworth's in 1930. After a period meeting at the YMCA they opened the Hawkey's Lane church on 11 June 1932, in time for the creation of the Methodist Union. It became home to a number branches of Methodism when the North Shields and Whitley Bay Circuits amalgamated in 1961.

Kennels Farm, 12 March 1931. Before Cleveland Road was carried through to this corner, the site was Camp Cottage. The farm was partly in occupation of T. Wears, coal merchant.

Hawkey's Lane, 12 March 1931. To the left, the original Preston Colliery pit heap was rebuilt as the cycle track in 1885. It became home to the colliery football team, later North Shields Athletic. Because of subsidence, Appleby Park was famous for McGarry's Hole. The High School is in the distance, opened in 1909.

Robert H. English, *c.* 1885. As a boy he was the star of the North Shields Amateur Bicycle Club, which built the cycle track. During a brief amateur career in Britain and the USA he won the World Championship. He turned professional around 1887. Retiring from racing after five years, he took the Corporation Arms pub, Linskill Street, where he died on 12 May 1897 aged thirty-four.

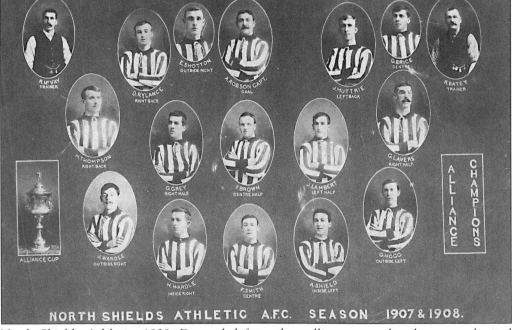

North Shields Athletic, 1908. Descended from the colliery team, they became a limited company in 1907. North Shields AFC was founded in 1929. Because of help the team received from fishmonger Joseph Appleby, the ground took his name.

Tynemouth Municipal High School, *c.* 1930. It became an adult education centre in 1973, on the opening of Norham High School.

High School, 1950. From left to right, back row: Roger Scott, Bill Black, ? Buglass, John Armstrong; George Thompson, Herbie Wakenshaw, John Arnold, David Huitson. Third row: Cathy Gibson, Pat Collins, Barbara Henderson, Miriam Loynes, Gayford White, Jean Wheldon, Eleanor Quenet. Second row: Audrey Southern, Margaret Pearson, Moira Wilson, Jean McAllum (?), Mr R. Hepple, Carol Hails, Janet Roughhead, Pamela McCarthy, Myra Mason. Front row: ? Matthews, Les Pearson, John Thompson, Bobby Hearn, -?-, George Southern (?), Gordon Limerick.

Coast Road Motor Co., 11 April 1956. The garage that opened with the Coast Road was extended in 1931. It was taken over in 1947 by Craven Bros of Monkseaton, who spent £40,000 remodelling the premises in 1966. It was the main Morris dealership in the area.

Queen Alexandra Road, c. 1905. The Kirton Park Building Estate began about 1902, and the main road took the name of the new Queen. The trees are probably those planted in February 1905. Benjamin Scott's shop was there until 1910.

Preston Cemetery,
10 April 1948. In 1850
the threatened closure
of the parish burial
ground led the council
to buy land outside
North Shields, seen to
the left. Anglican and
Nonconformist chapels
were built near the
centre. The cemetery
was laid out to provide
wooded walks, and
opened in 1856.

Crematorium,
13 September 1959.
The Anglican chapel
was adapted for the
purpose.

Foot's Carriage Works, *c. 1960*. Charles Foot set up the business in Preston village in 1851. In February 1876 he opened these purpose-built premises, employing fifty workers, and lived next door at Holly House. He developed a high reputation at home and abroad and after his death 1916 his sons continued as motor body builders. At the time of this picture it was a box factory.

Walton Avenue, *c. 1931*. In the background is a row of cottages at the west end of Front Street, Preston, since demolished.

Front Street, c. 1927. The Sportsman is in front of Foot's Buildings. The mock Tudor frontage was the idea of William Cawthorn, who owned the pub between 1896 and 1902. He was responsible for Cawthorn Terrace, the flats to the left.

The Sportsman Inn, c. 1967. One sportsman associated with the inn was Thomas Dixon, the publican during the First World War and up to his death in 1924. He was well known as a member of the North Shields Homing Society. His widow had the pub into the early 1930s.

Front Street, *c.* 1905. From 1862 to 1906 Moorcrest, to the left, was owned by the families of market gardener J.P. Turner and his grandson J.T. Smurthwaite. It was sold to Miss Potts of Chirton Grange Farm, who built Moorcrest Terrace next door. The porch and garden wall were recent additions.

Front Street, *c.* 1910. Price's grocery can be traced at 27/28 Front Street between 1886 and 1922.

Front Street, *c.* 1920. The Dymo soft drinks cart was once a familiar sight. About 1920 the McQueen cartwright shop, previously a smithy, became Gilbert Garner's garage. The Spread Eagle is almost opposite, with the white tiles of the Bambro' Castle beyond.

The Spread Eagle, *c.* 1967. The house already existed at the beginning of the nineteenth century. In 1934 it was in competition with the Bambro' Castle for the continuation of its licence. The latter lost and for a time it became William Thompson's fish and chip shop (see also p. 111).

Preston North Road, 10 April 1948. The main road passed Preston on the west side only. The Foxhunters Inn is hidden by the trees at the edge of the village. Later it moved north, close to the opencast mine in the distance. In the middle is Preston Grange Farm.

Coronation Day, June 1953. The villagers met in St Andrew's parish hall, at the beginning of Preston North Road.

The Home Guard, September 1940. The 11th Platoon 'C' Company of Tynemouth Home Guard were on a route march on Preston North Road. They were nicknamed the Baby Company, because it recruited among younger men.

Frank Currell Ltd, May 1958. Mr Currell's father had the Dun Cow, New York. The haulage business began at Preston about 1913. Frank was a founder member of the Road Haulage Association and of the village Chrysanthemum Society.

Foxhunters Inn, 1931. Early Victorian Shields folk spent summer Sundays walking to the market gardens at Preston. Thomas Craig, associated with Hogg's Gardens, opened the Foxhunters next to his orchard. Newcastle Breweries decided to close it in 1938.

Preston Grange Farm, 24 June 1957. At the 1649 enclosure Preston was divided into five farms. Originally Spearman's Marsh Farm, it was sold to the Duke of Northumberland in 1852. By that time it was held by Thomas Potts, whose family were there into the 1930s.

Preston Grange, *c.* 1965. In 1962 M.J. Liddell & Son proposed building a shopping and residential estate to rival Stockholm. The housing around Chiltern Road is part of the first stage. The Grangeway shopping centre followed, to the south. The first Presto supermarket was opened there 30 November 1967.

Tynemouth Technical School, *c.* 1959. The project was agreed in 1955 and lessons began in the building from 1959. In 1986 the Preston and Linskill High Schools were merged, and took the name John Spence School, in memory of John Foster Spence.

The Technical School, July 1959. From left to right, standing behind: J.A. Nichol; S.R. Nimmo; G. Grey, modern languages; R. Appleton; J.E.B. Pyle, English; G. Sanderson, science; P. Newton, workshop; Mrs A.E. Maling, clerk. Seated in front: Miss J. Dowling; Miss C. Snowden; Miss E. Appleby, housecraft; F.A. Whalley, deputy head; T.H.C. Walker, headmaster; Miss H. Nicholson, second mistress; Miss J. MacPhail; Miss M. Adams; Mrs Blowers.

Preston bypass, 31 May 1957. In October 1955 Tynemouth Council opted to drive Preston Road north, to co-ordinate with the building of the Technical School. Work began on 13 May 1957, to be completed on 14 November.

Front Street, 31 May 1957. A number of buildings were demolished in constructing the bypass. The old village smithy became the property of Ball Bros, builders and contractors, in the mid-1920s. William Ball served his time, before going on to run the business as W. Ball & Son.

Numbers 8 and 9 Argyle Place, 29 April 1946. Deputy Mayor R.A. Anderson officially opened the first two of a projected 2,500 post-war houses. At the left is the new MP, Miss Grace Colman. The builder was J.H.H. Rogers.

Preston Road, 1931. Ball & Son are visible in the distance. The pillars to the left are at the entrance to Preston Park. On the right is the gate to Tynemouth Vicarage. The picture may have been taken for the council scheme to widen the road.

Preston Park, *c*. 1958. John Fenwick once owned much of the land between Preston and North Shields. He built Preston House in 1818, seen here with the ATC Spitfire in the grounds. Preston Tower, at the north-east corner of the Park, was built by Edward Shotton in 1875. It was home to the Robinsons of the Stag Line from 1884 to 1939. At the south-west corner of the Park is The Elms, built for Richard Irvin about 1902.

Preston Road, c. 1895. From Preston Tower the tower of Christ Church is seen at the end of Preston Road; those of St Cuthbert's and the Memorial Methodist church are right and left. Kirton Park Farm rickyard is at the top right. The land was acquired in 1902 to build houses between Preston Road and Hawkey's Lane. Trees partially conceal the vicarage at the corner of Preston Avenue (previously Cut Throat Lane). Over their branches can be seen that part of the Tynemouth Union Workhouse which was extended over the town's Cricket Field during the 1880s.

Preston Avenue, *c.* 1905. Cut Throat or Cut Athwart Lane ran past Hogg's Gardens to Spital Dene Farm.

Preston Avenue, August 1949. The Borough Centenary flower show is being held on Percy Park Rugby Ground. Mr E. Rolls of North Shields won the Challenge Cup for the most successful entrant. At the foot of the picture are the King Edward Schools, opened in 1907.

King Edward Boys' School, 1924. In its first season they took the Benevolent & Orphans Fund Shield of the NUT. At the end of a competition prolonged by bad weather, they won the Tynemouth Schools League Cup and the Charity Bowl. In both finals their opponents were Percy Main.

King Edward Girls' School, 1948. Most of the girls are unidentified on the original print. Those known include Valerie Clark, Jacqueline Clazey, Jean Fay, Eleanor Quenette, Olga Steedman, Joan Vine, and Moira Wilson.

Trevor Terrace, *c.* 1931. The shops at the corner began to appear in trade directories in the early 1920s. To the left of the Trevor Stores is Albert Wilson, chemist, recently opened.

Trevor Terrace, *c.* 1930. Linskill Terrace is in the distance. C.W. Eskdale's hairdresser's shop pre-dated Mr Wilson. Beyond is S.W. Snaith's fried fish shop.

Preston Road, *c*. 1931. Through the 1920s the fishmonger's to the left was a branch of James Read & Sons. W.S. Crunden took the premises about 1928 and held them through the 1930s. The Jones & Barnsley fruit shop became Medhurst's around 1938.

Preston Road, *c*. 1930. Joseph Jones opened a branch of his grocery chain, to the left, by 1914. Charles Barnsley became a partner during the First World War. In the mid-1930s Jones & Barnsley became a limited company. The police call boxes went live on 21 January 1925.

118

Camp Terrace, 1967. The first four houses are alleged to have been built at the end of the Napoleonic Wars, for officers of the tented camps at South Preston.

Preston Hospital, 10 April 1941. The old workhouse took severe damage in one of the heaviest air raids. Doris Ewbank, an ambulance driver from Whitley Bay, was killed when the Holmlands building was hit.

Albion Road, 1921. The road is about to be widened by removing the wall and part of the burial ground at Christ Church.

Christ Church School, 1924. From left to right, back row: N. Hair, W. Potter, ? Scott, Bob Holme, K. Henry, John W. Parker, A. Iredale. Middle row: ? Smith, ? Errington, ? Cleator, John Henry Stanger (head of boys); Miss G.R. Martin (head of girls); E.E. Janson; ? Pearson. Front row (on ground): ? Arnott, Nancy Roxby, ? Hill. Mr Stanger was headmaster from 1911 to 1926; later he was the first head at Linskill School. Miss Martin arrived on 1 July 1924; Miss Janson retired on 31 August.

Previous page: Preston Road and Linskill Terrace, *c.* 1944. Preston Hospital is in the centre, Christ Church is to the left, and the Linskill Estate is at the bottom right.

Seven

Down to the River

Tynemouth Lodge, 1850s. In 1790 William Linskill moved into a new house north-east of the town. The lane to the west and north of his estate was known as Squire's Walk – later Linskill Terrace. The eastern boundary was Spital Dene. The house was demolished when the Linskills left in 1857.

Washington Terrace, *c.* 1910. It may have been an inconvenient mortgage which led Capt. Linskill to sell off the Tynemouth Lodge Estate. At the time the grounds were almost undeveloped, except for two houses at the northern end of Washington Terrace. The corner of Grey Street, to the left, was offered in 1861 as a capital site for a hotel.

King Edward Road, looking from the end of Washington Terrace towards Spital Dene Farm and Northumberland Park, *c.* 1930. The farmhouse, to the left, became the clubhouse when Tynemouth Golf Club was registered in July 1913.

Ancient Coffins. Northumberland Park, North Shields. 4280

St Leonard's Hospital, *c.* 1920. The stone coffins and other remains of a medieval hospital were discovered at the north end of Northumberland Park, when it was being laid out in 1884. The field gun was presented at the end of the First World War.

Northumberland Park, *c.* 1920. The greenhouses and aviaries were a notable feature of the park. The Smith family provided many of the gardeners.

125

Correction House Bank, *c.* 1980. This part of Tynemouth Road took its name from a court and lock-up, built in 1792. From 1907 it served as the Tynemouth & District Laundry. It is partly hidden by a house which had become the Tynemouth Lodge Hotel by 1821.

Percy Square, *c.* 1880. Towards the end of the Napoleonic Wars the Duke of Northumberland bought the barrack square, built in 1758. He built a massive stone wall at the riverside to defend the boulder clay cliffs from erosion. It was not a success, and by 1892 most of the south row had fallen.

"Sir James Knott Memorial Flats" North Shields. 11543

Knott's Flats, c. 1939. In January 1935 Tynemouth Council received a letter from the late Sir James Knott's trustees. They proposed building flats as a memorial to the ship-owner, who spent much of his life in the borough. They were to be of considerable architectural pretensions. The site selected was at Percy Square.

Sir James Knott Nursery, 3 November 1949.

Low Lights Dock, 22 June 1864. The riverside authorities turned out with great ceremony to lay the foundation stone for a deep water dock to replace the Black Middens below Percy Square. The scheme's failure led to the building of the North Shields Fish Quay and the Albert Edward Dock.

Toe wall, 21 March 1937. Repeated attempts to protect the cliffs failed. In the 1950s they were regraded at a shallower angle, almost to the walls of Knott's Flats. In the background is the Low Light at the Fish Quay.